Dragons of the Seven Cosmic Seas of ME

By Hildegarde Staninger
&
Roberto Mentuccia

© April 10, 2016

An Empress of the Sea Publication®

Copyright © 2016 by Hildegarde Staninger & Roberto Mentuccia

Dragons of the Seven Cosmic Seas of ME

by Hildegarde Staninger & Roberto Mentuccia

Printed in the United States of America.

ISBN 9781498485722

All rights reserved solely by the author. The author guarantees all contents are original and do not infringe upon the legal rights of any other person or work. No part of this book may be reproduced in any form without the permission of the author. The views expressed in this book are not necessarily those of the publisher.

Unless otherwise indicated, Scripture quotations taken from the New World Translation of the Holy Scriptures (NWT) is a translation of the Bible published by the Watch Tower Bible and Tract Society in 1961; it is used and distributed by Jehovah's Witnesses.

An Empress of the Sea Publication®

We come in Joy, PEACE and Eternal Happiness
Far from the Seven Cosmic Seas of ME
We are the Royal DRAGONS of ME.

Dedication

Over my life time I have seen many miracles that have opened my heart to always have hope and faith in my fellow man. And as a father who loves his children I dedicate this book to my daughter, Marisa and my son, Marco as well as to my son-in-law, Scott and my granddaughter, Luca. I wish all of them greatness, strength and courage as they go on their own journey of life in search of unconditional love.

                        Roberto Mentuccia
                        April 12, 2016

Dedication

Over the years of my life, I have felt the movement of the sands of time. Time passes through the Ages, but the sands that my ancient ancestors walked on during their lifetimes are the same. It was there for the present and past relatives of mine as well as for your own. I, myself, have believed in the simple purity of the senescence of the "Dragons of the Seven Cosmic Seas of ME." And I know that their sound and light from the Most High God will be shown to have been always deep within each of our own hearts.

My own work as a scientist has seen the many realities of science through the passage of time. And as I walk on my own path on the sands of time, I have forged my own Destiny. The sands of time are only a reflection of the cosmic dust of all of the Ages of the Eons of Life, to become the speck of Divine Creation within each and every one of us. And with these thoughts, I dedicate this book to my own beautiful creation, my daughter Aurora.

Dr. Hildegarde Staninger®
April 12, 2016

Dragons of the Seven Cosmic Seas of ME

Table of Contents

Preface
Dragons of the Seven Cosmic Seas of ME
The Royal Dragons of the Kingdom of ME
Here is Our Story
Hils ~ I AM the Crystal Emerald
Shar Nil ~ I AM the Crystal Carnelian
Li Li Lo ~ I AM the Crystal Beryl
Como ~ I AM the Crystal Lapis
Zomo ~ I AM the Crystal Carnelian
Ba Shi ~ I AM the Crystal Topaz
Zami ~ I AM the Crystal Jasper
Ti Pi ~ I AM the Crystal Chrysolite
Te Ami ~ I AM the Crystal Onyx
Ka Mui ~ I AM the Crystal Amethyst
Jin Dar Mi ~ I AM the Crystal Sapphire
Unseen Brother Dragon Number 1 ~ I AM the Crystal Carbuncle
Unseen Brother Dragon Number 2 ~ I AM the Crystal Tigers Eye
Dragon Eyes ~ I AM the Crystal Carbuncle and Jade
To Be the End or Not to Be the End
Dragon Fruit

Preface

In the beginning of ALL BEGINNINGS there was darkness
And out of darkness came light and out of light
came the sound and the birth of the
Dragons of the Seven Cosmic Seas of ME.

Dragons of the Seven Cosmic Seas of ME

Long, long ago there was a noble royal race of Dragons that flew from one universe to another. They took commands only from the Empress of the Dragons, who ruled all of the cosmos of Spirit as ordained by God, which was known as the Seven Cosmic Seas of ME.

The Empress was known throughout the kingdom as God's number one warrior from the Seven Cosmic Seas of ME. She was known for allowing her thoughts to command the Dragons of ME. And through her thoughts, the Dragons would receive their messages and travel throughout the different kingdoms of the many worlds of the cosmos, bringing neutrality to all as the supreme equalizer of the energies for all the EONS of Time, Space and Eternity.

The Dragons of ME were known for their great connection, not only to the Empress of the Dragons of the Seven Cosmic Seas of ME, but for their resonance to the single individual specks of dust within the heart of God himself.

The Empress of the Dragons with her Dragon Green Jade eyes would take care of God's special gardens. God's gardens were very unique throughout the Cosmos, because their flowers and fruit would be made of precious stones – CRYSTALS.

It has been said that the Crystals would be treasured throughout the Seven Cosmic Seas of ME, because they were the true reflection of a single tear of a Human Being on Earth as found in the Milky Way. For, it was known by all in the cosmos that a single Human's Tear would form a blending of all of their own crystals of creation. The Crystals of Creation were known as the "ME's of God", the physical re-emergence of his presence throughout all of eternity, as well as, through the portals of space and time. The crystal flowers and fruit of God's gardens would grow in all shapes and colors. The precious stones of God's reflective heart were known on Earth and throughout the Seven Cosmic Seas of ME. They were made into the dust found in each and every one of All Living Beings' hearts. A single speck of dust from any of the sacred gardens of God would be used by God to create the crystal lattice of creation for YOU, as well as anything he desired in his heart. A sprinkle of the dust even created all of the Cosmos through all the Ages of Life on Earth, the Heavens and many other Worlds of Creation.

The gardens' crystals would come in various shapes and sizes, which were known for their eternal spiritual beauty. The precious stones would then form into each of the following precious stones, and even more would be made by God. It was known throughout the Kingdom of ME that God would make many more crystals; for, he would use his thoughts to make them into BEING with all his heart and mind's eye – Creation.

Carnelian, Topaz, and Jasper.
Chrysolite, Beryl and Onyx.
Sapphire, Carbuncle, Lapis and Emerald.

And from the time of their creation, each of the stones' fruits would then be guarded by the Sacred Royal Dragons of the Kingdom of ME found in the Seven Cosmic Seas.

The Royal Dragons of the Kingdom of ME

The Royal Dragons of the Kingdom of ME lived on the holy mountains of God as you passed through the Seven Cosmic Seas of ME. They would burn an eternal fire of God's eternal love to have within each and every heart created by God throughout all of the Cosmos.

The mountains would be found on various planets throughout the Universes of the Cosmos. And each Dragon would wait their turn to be called by the Empress of the Dragons to send peace and joy through the worlds of Heaven and Beyond.

It was also known that for each crystal stone that was a "TRUE" ME, it would contain the perfect resonances of sound and light from the very heart of God himself.

The crystal stones would be made into dust, and each Dragon of ME would carry their dust throughout the Cosmos for their Sound and Light to be sung throughout the Cosmos. The Dragons of ME would sing a song of praise to the Most High God throughout the Worlds of Creation. And as they sang their praise, each Dragon of Me would descend from the Heavens and shine their light of gold, red, blue, green, purple, orange and indigo black with their "Humming of the Ages" as their eternal song of songs from God to All of Creation.

It has been known throughout the reflection of Time that each Dragon of ME would become a Mighty Guardian known as "the Great One Who Metes Out the Fates." And some would be the watchers of the forests, seas and sky of Nature as they would guard ALL of the Cosmos for the True One's coming.

Here is Our Story

We are the Sacred Royal Dragons of the Seven Cosmic Seas of ME.
All of us have come here to you, so you will read the story of each of us,
the Thirteen Sacred Royal Dragons of ME. We were born in the Seven
Cosmic Seas of ME and will travel all of the worlds of the universes to
bring each of you the dust of creation as we tell you
our very own story of BEING.

Hils

I am Hils, the Dragon who guards the Royal Staff
of the Empress of the Dragons.
I am the one who shines the orders of the Cosmos, Heavens and Planets to hear and see the Divine within all of God's Creation.
I awaken the spiritually deaf and blind, so my Brother Dragons will send their own light for ALL to hear the sound of the Light of God.
I guard the Emerald dust found in the Divine Heart of God.

I AM the Crystal Emerald Hils

My color is emerald green. And if you look very closely you will see sometimes "red emerald." It has been told that I provide for domestic bliss and instill sensitivity and loyalty within your heart chakra as it radiates your own rays to others.
I will enhance your memory and stimulate your greater mental capacity.
I will help you to combine intelligence and discernment which allows you to make the "right" choice of your intent and others' actions.
If you see the red hues of my deep emerald cosmic seas within my own crystal, then you will know me as BIXBITE. And I will come to you with my rays of light and sound from the constellations of Taurus, Gemini and Aries.
I AM the Crystal Emerald, which is known to be the "Precious Stone of Successful Love."

Shar Nil

I am Shar Nil, the Dragon guardian of the Sound of the Universe.
I glisten and reflect the light of God's Seven Rays to make the perfect tones known as the "Seven Spheres of the Universe." A single sphere will move their perfect tone to form a dimension of possibilities that will radiate from the faith one has deep within their own heart.
I AM the guardian of the crystal Carnelian; the dust found in the Divine Heart of God.

I AM the Crystal Carnelian Shar Nil

My color ranges from white to yellow and even from a white color to a red. My individual crystal dust forms the shape of a hexagon.
I am known throughout the Seven Cosmic Seas of ME as the "ELIXIR" that purifies a Being and their surroundings.
I am the agent of the Most High that calms One and purifies their soul as I provide the connective "thread" between the intellectual mind, spirit and life's quickening.
I am the one that allows a Being to Dance on the "Razor's Edge of Life" as my Brother's and I bring forth the fruition of your work.
The single word that describes me is ELOQUENCE as I travel from the constellation of Aries to aid you in your vibrations of life.

Li Li Lo

I am Li Li Lo, the Dragon who guards all of the
Dimensions of Time and Space.
My own crystal is known for its special crystalline lattice, in which my
own perfection will allow me to change time and allow me to jump
through the Past, Present and Future of Time itself
within a blink of a Human's eye.
I AM the guardian of the crystal Beryl - the dust found
in the Divine Heart of God.

I AM the Crystal Beryl
Li Li Lo

My crystallized structures form a prism of all crystal forms. I can change my form into many other forms that are known to be aquamarine, bixbite, emerald, goshenite, heliodor, morganite, and yellow golden beryl. When I am the Golden Beryl, my crystals are of a royal and old universal ray of light - the light that brings forth each and every Ancestor of your own Being.
I travel to you from the golden rays that are found in the constellation Leo.
I bring to you all forms of purity from every plane and dimension of the Universes of Time and Space.
I am your TRUE Potential, which paves the way for your initiative and independent spirit of thought, word and deeds.
I instill within the little pyramid-like faces of my crystals the GUIDANCE from the source of ALL LIFE within CREATION.

Como

I am Como, the Dragon who guards the Eternal Flame within God's heart. I am made out of the dust of Lapis, which is throughout God's Divine Heart.
I have protected every ruler on Earth in hope that they would have a heart of Divine Justice. For it has been known, that each and every one of them would have their seeds tested by Father Time. Some have passed their test and some have not, for their Ancient Ancestors know the truths within their hearts and pray for their eternal redemption.

I AM the Crystal Lapis Como

My color is the deep blue of all the Universes that
were created long before Time was born.
I provide to you the quickening and energy needed to open your throat and
the third eye chakras. I stimulate the wisdom and
perfection of your Being within.
I am known as the precious stone of Total Awareness as
I release information from above to You.
I am the key to planetary knowledge and the stone of the Kings and
Queens of your world known as Earth.
The angel of the Lord Most High gave my crystal as a ring to King
Solomon, who was known to be the greatest precious stone wearer of
"ALL on Earth." He would use my crystal that was given to him by God
in his ring - the ring which he would use to control legions of demons as
they would build his temple.
And I Purify, Correct and Rectify the damage created by Mankind as a
simple man or ruler of Earth, as well as your own internal and
external environment upon your RNA and DNA.
The Eternal Book of God's Creation is within You.

Zomo

I am Zomo, the Dragon who guards Mother Eternity.
Eternity will always exist as Time does, for they are eternally in love throughout the universe. Their love is unconditional love that becomes the seeds of time bearing witness to the de-activation of jealously, hatred, poverty and unjust acts as committed throughout
the Seven Seas of the Cosmos.
I guard the Carnelian dust found in the Divine Heart of God.

I AM the Crystal Carnelian Zomo

My colors are in a uniform hue of red, orange and red-brown.
I am the crystal that brings forth your analytical and
precision attributes into this world and the next.
I am the crystal whose rays protect Beings against envy, fear and rage,
and I help to ease the tears of deep sorrow.
I aid One in balancing their emotions and their
physical worlds in this one and the next.
I am known throughout the Seven Cosmic Seas of ME for my power to
dispel apathy, indolence and passivity.
I instill deep within You that tiny spark of INQUISITIVENESS.

Ba Shi

I am Ba Shi, the Dragon who guards all Warriors of God, and my heart is filled with the PEACE within God's own heart.
I have many prisms that hang from me, for each of my prisms shines their light of the Savior to the Warrior who will become like no other.   This Warrior of God will stand for the presence of Eternal Peace and shine their light for all warriors to follow to the path of PEACE on Earth,
the Heavens and Beyond.
I guard the golden light of the dust Topaz as found
in the Divine Heart of God.

I AM the Crystal Topaz Ba Shi

My fellow Dragon Brothers know me for my Joyfulness. My colors are
many and range from pink, green red,
gold, yellow, blue, white, red-yellow,
brown, grey, to even colorless.
The Colorless One is known to be the equal to my brother Te Ami, for he
is the crystal Onyx. It is known to be among
my rarest crystal form on Earth.
I travel to you from the constellation of Sagittarius
through the Milky Way.
I am known as the precious stone of TRUE Love with success
in ALL of One's Endeavors.
I AM the Conductor of the Universe as I direct your
deepest desires to MANIFEST into REALITY.

Zami

I am Zami, the Dragon who guards "Self-Love" within all living Beings of the One TRUE Light.

Self-Love is not made of EGO, but a reflection of the True One's one love for self within each of us. The one being, YOU are a single speck of dust – a true piece of God's own heart within your own heart.

It has been said throughout Time Eternal, that if you do not love yourself in equal balance with God's own heart through your own heart, you will spin into chaos for all eternity. Be still and feel the love within your own heart for I am here to help you open your heart as a chick opens its shell.

I guard the Jasper dust found in the Divine Heart of God.

I AM the Crystal Jasper Zami

My colors are many and of various shapes. I can come to you as the spots of a leopard or the bands on a lizard. The hues of my rays of color come to you as dark red, orange, yellow, tan, brown, green, grey, and even blue.
I am the SUPREME NURTURER of ALL Life as I bring Joy and Prosperity and Release you from your Earthly bonds.
I am the guardian of the solar plexus chakra that has brought forth the old ways of Earth's Native American Indians.
I travel to you from the constellation of Leo, and I am your connection to the AFTER WORLDS of Space and Time throughout
Yours and your Ancestors' lives.
My favorite colors of my crystal light are light to dark green when I am known as the Lizard Stone – JASPER from Gemini.

Ti Pi

I am Ti Pi, the Dragon who is the guardian of HOPE. I am smaller than my Brothers, but I move with the agility of a cat to bring forth HOPE within each and every heart of MANKIND.

Hope is deep within the heart, and when Hope and Faith are present, the grounding rod is formed to God. The rod is the Staff of the Empress of the Dragon, which will shine through your own hope as her light will shine upon your own heart's dust, so you will blend with God's shining light and become the BRIGHTEST Heavenly Body for the Kingdoms of Heaven and Earth to see.

I guard the Chrysolite dust found in the Divine Heart of God.

I AM the Crystal Chrysolite Ti Pi

My crystal colors are known throughout the Seven Cosmic Seas of ME. They are green-white, olive-green, green, green-black, yellow and brown, brown-yellow, brown-red, and even white. I may be deadly to Mankind on the planet Earth for my crystals are flexible and separate into delicate fibers which may pierce into their organs known as lungs and stomach.

I am the BONDER as I assist One in finding the TRUE SELF by clearing all the unknown, unseen and physical BAGGAGE in One's Past, Present and Future. And I have the special gift from the Most High to even clear the baggage of One's Ancestors as long as a single relative of theirs desires it to occur.

I will expand your TELEPATIC Endeavors in both sending and receiving information and messages from other planes within your plane.

I am the cousin to Eternity who uses the number 8 to signify her presence, and I am the Master of the number 55.

Te Ami

I am Te Ami, the Mightiest Dragon of all my Brother Dragons of ME. I am the guardian of the "Spirit of the Most High."

The Spirit of the Most High is within each and every living creature throughout the Cosmos. And on Earth, Mankind has been deemed by God to be the Steward to his creation, the Animals.

I guard the dust of Onyx within God's heart. Black "Yes" is the Onyx, but through its prism lattice there is a convergence of all of the colors of light that form the ONE color Black, for black is known as "No Light."

I guard the Onyx dust found in the Divine Heart of God.

I AM the Crystal Onyx Te Ami

My rays of color are black, black and white, red and white, orange-brown with a touch of honey and white. I can come in the form of many other rays of the SPECTRUMS of Sound and Light.
I travel with my Brothers from the constellation of Leo to bring to you Self-Control, the Power of Wisdom, the Encouragement of Happiness and GOOD FORTUNE.
My nickname throughout the Seven Cosmic Seas of ME is "Cookie" because I am known to eat a Fortune Cookie or two as found on Earth.
My Brothers and I have reverence to your Ancient Scholars for they brought forth Astronomy as they named a constellation after my Brothers and Me, the Dragons of the Seven Cosmic Seas of ME.
You know the constellation as DRACO – the Dragon.

Ka Mui

I am Ka Mui, the Dragon of the Guardians of Nature.
The Worlds of Heaven and the Beyond know of me throughout the Cosmos of Life as I exist in its natural form - PURITY. Sacred is the purity of its fruit and that is why I am assigned to shine my light for all to see the Beauty of Creation within the deepness of One's Heart.
I guard the Amethyst dust found in the Divine Heart of God.

I AM the Crystal Amethyst Ka Mui

My radiant rays of color will shine throughout many constellations that join the Seven Cosmic Seas of ME – Pisces, Virgo, Aquarius and Capricorn.

You will always remember me for I am the little tickle in your throat and the calmness within your Heart of All Hearts.

My favorite color ray is purple, and I can shine in many forms because the more manganese that I have present, the lighter my ray will become. And this is even true for when my crystal becomes the deep and dark purple ray when you will find iron deep within its core.

I am known as the BRINGER of ENERGY to balance the energies of intellectual, emotion, and physical bodies as I provide the clear pathway between the Earth plane and all the other Worlds of Heaven and Beyond to Bare Witness.

The Most High One allows me to bring to each and every one of You, "PERFECT PEACE" as the BESTOWER of ETERNAL PEACE.

Jin Dar Mi

I am Jin Dar Mi, the Hidden Dragon. I have two older Dragon Brothers that help me to "Guard All of Humanity" throughout the Seven Seas of the Cosmos.

My Brothers and I are always at God's beck and call, to help all who are on the path to, and of eternal, unconditional love and peace. On Earth there is a fruit in our shape because it looks like the heart of God. It is known by your World as the PEACH, another symbol of God's peace for the hearts of MANKIND to share.

I guard the Sapphire dust found in the Divine Heart of God.

Unseen Brother Dragon Number 1 is the guardian of the Quartz and Carbuncle dust found in the Divine Heart of God.

And our other brother, Unseen Brother Dragon Number 2, is the guardian of the Tiger's Eye dust found in the Divine Heart of God.

I AM the Crystal Sapphire Jin Dar Mi

My crystals form tubes and hexagonal double pyramid structures as they
send out their rays of white, black, purple, yellow and green.
I radiate throughout every Being's single universe called the CELL.
I bring to you all of the stars of the universe's radiance through a
single speck of dust of my crystal's own light.
I am known throughout the Seven Cosmic Seas of ME
as the precious stone of PROSPERITY.
I travel to you from the constellations of Virgo, Libra and Sagittarius, and
my perfect sound is "tooooooooo."

I AM the Crystal Quartz and Carbuncle Unseen Brother Dragon Number 1

My colors are many because I can come to you as the crystal Quartz or Carbuncle. You know the other name for me as Ruby when I am Carbuncle which is the Old Timer's name for me.
When I am Quartz my color is CLEAR, and I can make the other colors expand their masses, gains, druses and prisms of hexagons. I come forth as the rays of rose, smoky browns, yellow and light purple.
I have been used by many a DIVINE Power to bring forth the energy of the stars into the soul.
I have another name CLARITY.
I AM the Crystal CARBUNCLE – I am the color of a Human's Blood as I travel from the constellations of Leo, Scorpio, Cancer and Sagittarius. When I am not the color of a Human's Blood on Earth, I AM the rays of pink, crimson red and orange-red as I display my star-like luminosity through the transmission of ALL LIGHT from Heaven and Beyond.
I am the ONE who ENCOURAGES BLISS.

I AM the Crystal Tiger's Eye Unseen Brother Dragon Number 2

My color rays are blue and gold as I travel to You from the constellation of Capricorn. Capricorn is very special to my Brothers and Me for it is of water and land just as Creation deemed through his heart.

Through the Ages of Time my color range has included red, brown, gold, cream, black and blue. I am known as the Big Tiger Dragon, because my eyes do not shine straight like the Cats of Earth. They burst forth like an exploding star, so that all will remember the birth of BEING.

I am known as the BRINGER of LIGHT to the Earthly Peoples through the "River of Humanity" so their journey to the TRUE ONE will be easier.

Dragon Eyes

I am Dragon Eyes, the Supreme Guardian of the Royal Dragons of ME and commanding Admiral of the Seven Cosmic Seas.

My Dragons and I guard and protect ALL of God's Creations throughout the Seven Cosmic Seas, which are part of the SEVEN Rays of God's own Light.

I have been given the task of protecting the Royal Dragons of ME for all Time and throughout ALL of ETERNITY's Divine Unconditional Love from GOD to You, his most beautiful creation from deep within his own heart.

It has been said through the Ages of Time that God gave you a sacred message to remember deep within your heart. His message to you, his most Beloved Creation is the following:

"NOW is the time for all creation to hear these words that will awaken your heart and put stillness deep within your mind's eye.

Guard yourself, Heal yourself and have FAITH and HOPE within yourself. And know that I am within the DUST of your own heart, and at any time you can be "ONE" with the Most High; you will manifest your own true light as it shines throughout the Seven Cosmic Seas of Creation's WILL for PEACE and Unconditional Love, just as I did in the Beginning, and just as You and I will shine our sound of sounds and light of lights in the End.

The white light of Carbuncle will shine deep within the lattice of your own crystal dust within your heart. It will shine your light to ME – The Creator of Heaven and Earth and throughout the Seven Cosmic Seas of ME. You will become the BEACON of Light for all to gather and shine their own light throughout the Worlds of HEAVENS and BEYOND.

For deep within the Seven Seas of your own heart, the "TRUTH" will rise up upon the waves of Time. You will always know I am always within your HEART, for you will now SHINE your own true light of being throughout all of the Cosmos to see and reflect."

I guard the Carbuncle dust found in the Divine Heart of God, because my eyes are truly made of the Green Jade of ALL the Ancient Ones.

I AM the Crystal Carbuncle and Jade Dragon Eyes

My Dragon, Unseen Brother Dragon Number 1, has told you about our crystal Carbuncle. This crystal when combined with my precious crystal of Green Jade is among the most powerful of the DIVINE REALM for all to share.

If a Human lays their head upon my crystal of Green Jade, they will fall asleep and that is why I am known as the DREAM STONE of FIDELITY as I bring forth the realization of one's own potential and devotion to one's TRUE purpose. I am the real crystal of the Sands of Time that creates One's Own DESTINY.

I am the VISION deep within your heart and unseen eyes that will awaken the spiritually blind and deaf.

Hear my words for you are ALL Blessed Upon the CREATION of the Most High GOD and will always be a kindred spirit of his eternal flame within your own heart.

To BE the END or Not to BE the END

Our story of the "Dragons of the Seven Cosmic Seas of ME" has come to its end, but for the ONES who do not believe in this story and the legends of old about fellow Dragons with all their heart;
then, all you will have to do is to remember that God gave to all of the Royal Dragons of the Kingdom of ME something very special for all of the Beings of Earth to always remember them by – the Dragon Fruit.

Dragon Fruit

I am called by my name Dragon Fruit. If you look real close you will know that the Spirit of a Dragon is born out of a Dragon Fruit on Earth. In the quiet areas of where you may have grown up, you will remember the quiet and never-changing patterns of life that occurred there. For, in these areas of the world is where the Empress of the Dragon hides the Dragon Eggs of the FUTURE, so that we will be able to send the light of the Most High God throughout every REALM of CREATION.

I hope you will enjoy eating a piece of my fruit as found on the planet Earth. Chemists of Earth say I am high in vitamin C and many minerals. And remember, minerals are what make up the dust of crystals for them to shine their LIGHT and SOUND throughout You and the various WORLDS of the UNIVERSES of Heaven and Beyond. And even in the Seven Cosmic Seas of ME where the DRAGONS of ME live, you will find them in ETERNAL HARMONY with the Empress of the Dragon – Dragon Eyes, as they await the call of God to spread his Divine Heart's dust throughout the Dimensions of Time and Space.

Ecclesiastes 3:17-22

17 I myself have said in my heart. "The [true] God will judge the righteous one and the wicked one, for there is time for every affair and concerning every work there." **18** I, even I, have said in my heart with regard to the sons of mankind that the [true] God is going to select the, that they may see that they themselves are beasts. **19** For there is an eventuality as respects the sons of mankind and as respects the beast and they have the same eventuality. As the one dies, so the other dies, and they all have but one spirit, so that there is no superiority of the man over beast, for everything is vanity. **20** All are going to one place. They have all come to be from the dust, and they are all returning to the dust. **21** Who is there knowing the spirit of the sons of mankind, whether it is ascending upward; whether it is ascending downward to the earth? **22** And I have seen that there is nothing better than that the man should rejoice in his works, for that is his portion, because who will bring him in to look on what is going to be after him?

About the Authors

Dr. Hildegarde Staninger is an Industrial Toxicologist/IH and Doctor of Integrative Medicine. She has authored other books and articles in the applied sciences and engineering, occupational health and safety, and environment as well as the creative arts and educational study guides for occupational certification programs.

Roberto Mentuccia is a Holistic Nutritionist and Certified IEIA H-SCADA BioEnergy Field Professional. He specializes in the use of nutrition through applied photophonic cellular resonance as addressed in DNA Linguistics and Cellular Communication. And this is the first time Mr. Mentuccia has collaborated with Dr. Staninger on this special book entitled <u>Dragons of the Seven Cosmic Seas of ME</u>.

Notes

Notes

Notes

Notes

www.ingramcontent.com/pod-product-compliance
Lightning Source LLC
LaVergne TN
LVHW020416070526
838199LV00054B/3635